Elizabeth and the Potato Dolly

By Barbara Sorensen Fallick

Photos by Amelia Thelin

Copyright © 2013 Barbara Fallick—All rights reserved.

No part of this book may be reproduced in any manner without the author's express written consent, except in the case of brief excerpts in critical reviews and articles. Inquires about this book should be addressed to:

Barbara Fallick
goldstreetpublishers@gmail.com
Website: GoldStreetPublishers.com

Layout and additional photography:
Melody Wilson Young
graphicdesignbymelody.com

ISBN-13: 978-0-9997020-0-0

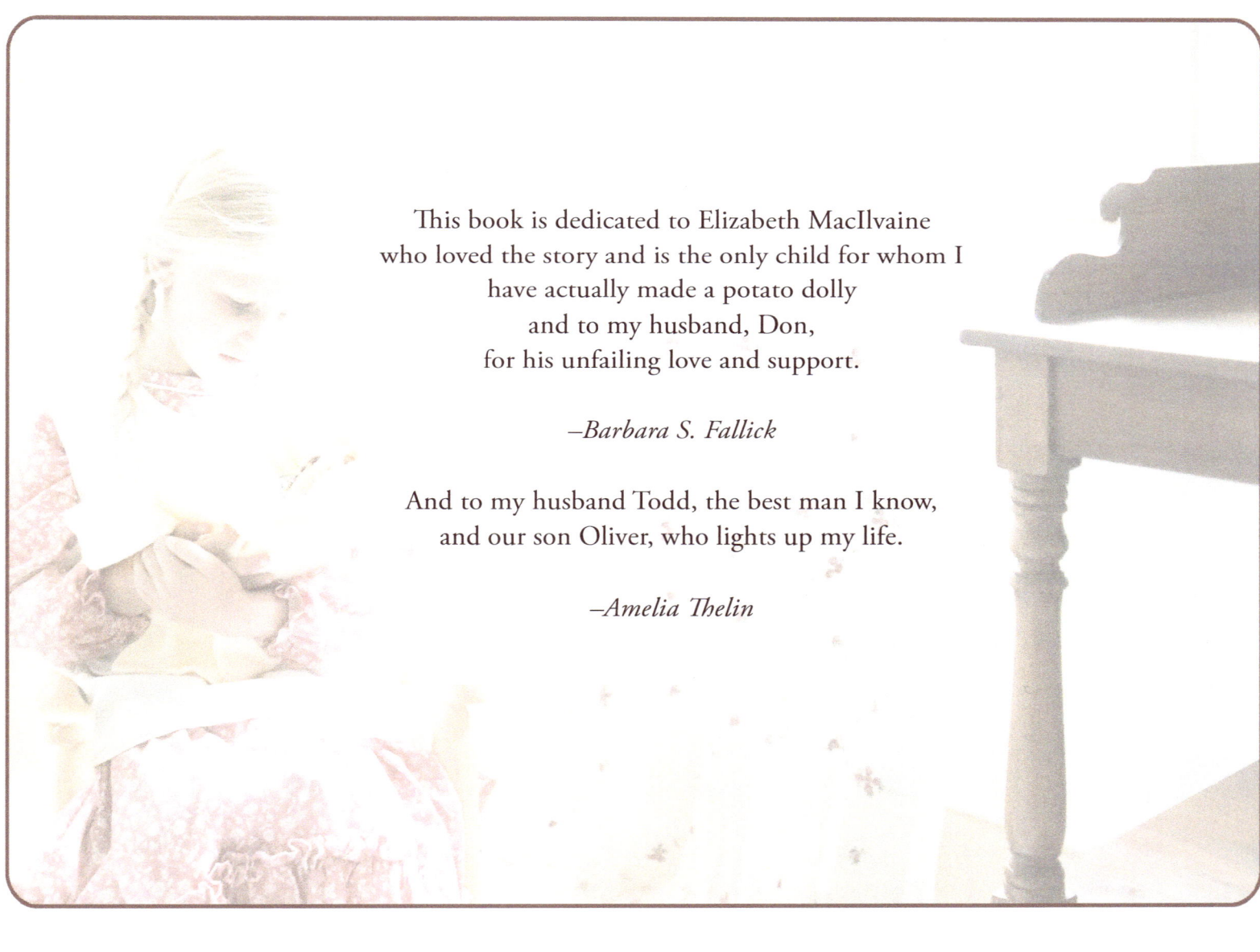

This book is dedicated to Elizabeth MacIlvaine
who loved the story and is the only child for whom I
have actually made a potato dolly
and to my husband, Don,
for his unfailing love and support.

–Barbara S. Fallick

And to my husband Todd, the best man I know,
and our son Oliver, who lights up my life.

–Amelia Thelin

Lydia was five-and-a-half when she started school in 1917.
Most children did not start school until they were six,
but Lydia started at five-and-a-half, because her Poppa was the teacher.

The other children at school called Poppa "Mr. Marchant".
They were in first, second, fourth, fifth, and sixth grades.
No one was in the third grade because no one in the school was that age.

Thomas was the only other first grader. He was six years old.
Lydia thought Thomas was awfully handsome,
but she never dared tell him. She never dared talk to him at all.

One day Poppa said, as Poppa often did,
"Who would like to tell us a story?"

Lydia raised her hand.
Poppa called on Lydia to tell the class a story.

"Once upon a time," Lydia began,
"there was a little girl named Elizabeth.

Her Mama said, 'Elizabeth, will you please go to the cellar and fetch some potatoes for Poppa's dinner?'
'Yes, Mama,' said Elizabeth, and she took her bucket from its nail and went to the cellar.

Mama laid the fire to cook the potatoes.

Elizabeth had not returned when she finished.

Mama went to
the door and called,
'Eliiiii-zabeth.

Elizabeth did not answer,
and Elizabeth did not come.

Mama swept the floor.

Elizabeth had not returned when she finished.

Mama went to the porch and called, 'Eliiiii-zabeth.'
Elizabeth did not answer, and Elizabeth did not come.

Mama set the dishes on the table.
Elizabeth had not returned when she finished.

Mama went to the yard
and called,
'Eliiiii-zabeth.'

Elizabeth did
not answer,
and Elizabeth did
not come.

Mama went down into
the cellar to see what was
keeping Elizabeth.

There was Elizabeth, sitting on
a barrel, rocking a potato
and singing a lullaby:

'Bye, Baby, Bye Low
Bye, Baby, Bye Low
Bye, Baby, Bye Low
Bye, Baby, Bye'

'Elizabeth!' Mama was cross.
'Didn't you hear me calling you?
I was getting worried
when you didn't answer.'

'I'm sorry, Mama,
but I found a potato dolly.'

'Elizabeth, you must always
answer when your mother calls.'

'I know. I'm sorry, Mama. I will."

'Elizabeth,' said Mama, 'I'll get the potatoes cooking, and then we'll make that into a proper potato dolly.'

When Mama had the potatoes cooking for Poppa's dinner, she got out raisins and toothpicks. Elizabeth made eyes and a smile on the potato dolly.

Then Mama
helped Elizabeth make
yellow braids from
crochet thread,
with pink ribbon bows,
for the potato dolly.

Next, they made a
blue print dress and
a white apron
and put it on the
potato dolly.

Finally, Mama gave
Elizabeth a scrap of
yellow flannel
from the piece basket
for a blanket.
Elizabeth wrapped her
potato dolly in the flannel.

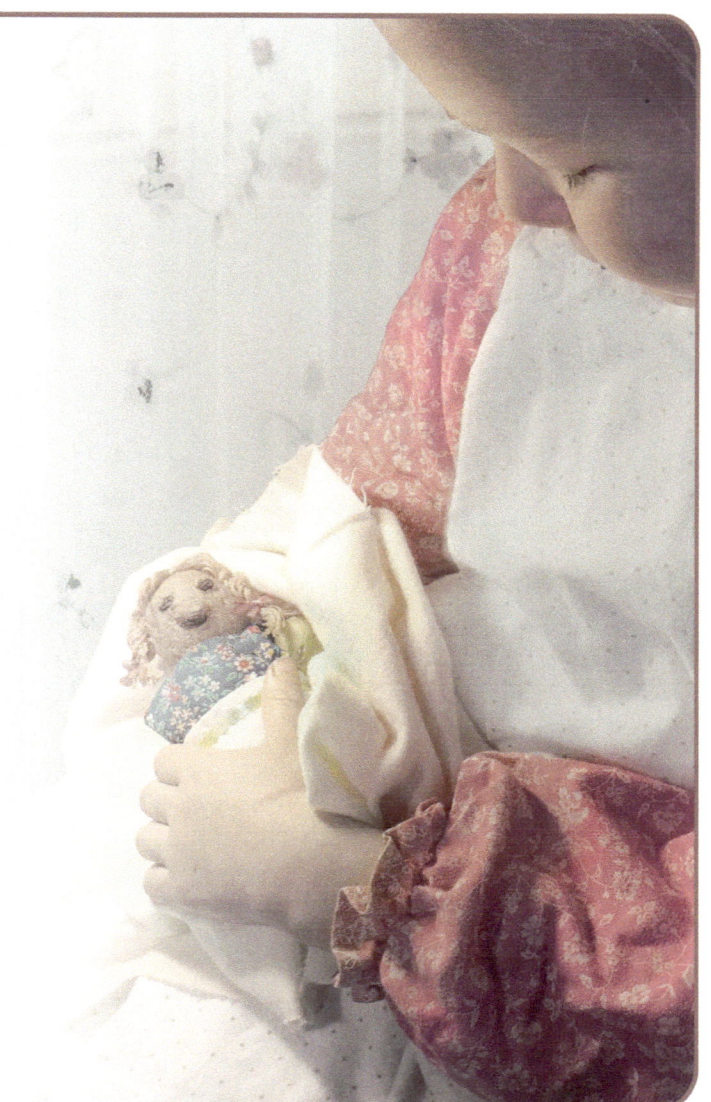

When Poppa came in, he was surprised.
'You have a new baby!" he said.

While he washed up for dinner,
Elizabeth sat in the rocker Poppa had made for her
and rocked her potato dolly and sang:

'Bye, Baby, Bye Low
Bye, Baby, Bye Low
Bye, Baby, Bye Low
Bye, Baby, Bye'

"Mr. Marchant," said one of the big girls,
"let's always let the little kids tell the stories."

"Lydia, I have never heard the story of the potato dolly," said Poppa.
"Where did you hear it?"

"Mama told me, Poppa."

When the children went out for recess, Thomas asked Lydia,
"Did Elizabeth have blue eyes?"
"I don't know," said Lydia.
"My sister Elizabeth has blue eyes." said Thomas.

Lydia felt as warm on the inside as the bright sunshine on the outside.
She wanted to dance and hug herself.
Thomas had talked to her!

Agnes Taylor Marchant, the author's grandmother, was born of pioneer stock in Salt Lake City, Utah in 1881. She was of English heritage and her grandfather was John Taylor, the third prophet of the Church of Jesus Christ of Later-day Saints. She told her daughters the story of "Elizabeth and the Potato Dolly." No one knows the origin of the story.

Lydia Taylor Marchant, the author's mother, is portrayed by her great-granddaughter Lydia Shannon.

The incident in the one room school house actually happened as told to the author by her mother.

Robert Henry Casper Marchant is portrayed by Avram Richard Shannon, Lydia's father.

Elizabeth is portrayed by Roxanne Sloan, the author's grand-daughter and her mother by Halley Miranda, the author's daughter.

A special thanks to the children in the classroom.
They served as volunteers at This Is The Place Heritage Park in Salt Lake City, summer 2011.

  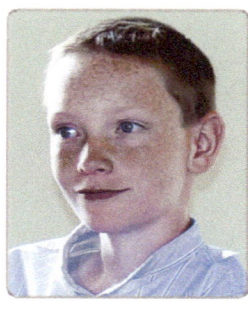  

Ryker Tureson · Emery Tureson · Keegan Tureson · Mia Tureson · Emma Gleason

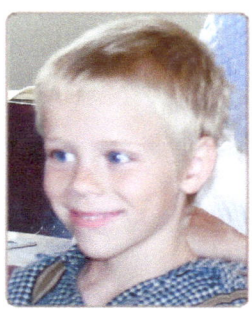    

Seth Hall · Billy Hall · Lydia Wells · Nathaniel Wells · Lizzy Lee
Additional Model

The Author

Barbara Sorensen Fallick grew up in Emery and Manti, Utah. She is the mother of a blended family of 10 children, and proud grandma to 40 grandchildren. She spends a lot of her time doing family history and preserving it for future generations. She, with many of her grandchildren, have volunteered at This is the Place State Park in Salt Lake City, Utah. She is a member of the Daughters of the Utah Pioneers and Daughters of the American Revolution.

The Photographer

Amelia Thelin has enjoyed photography on a semi-professional basis for over 10 years. She currently resides in Salt Lake City, Utah, with her husband and son. This is her first experience as a photo-illustrator.

www.ingramcontent.com/pod-product-compliance
Lightning Source LLC
Chambersburg PA
CBHW041749290426

44113CB00004B/100